WAITING WORLD

CELEBRATING ADVENT WITH THE SAINTS

I also learned, despite language, sometimes wisdom finds us in others, traditions. M.

LIGHTS FOR A WAITING WORLD

CELEBRATING ADVENT WITH THE SAINTS

Silas S. Henderson

ABBEY PRESS Publications

ISBN 978-0-87029-686-4

Library of Congress 2015947446

Copyright ©2015 Silas S. Henderson

Published by Abbey Press Publications
1 Hill Drive, St. Meinrad, IN 47577
Printed by Abbey Press in United States of America.
www.abbeypresspublications.com

Contents

✣

This book is dedicated to Father Gavin Barnes, O.S.B.

*Be patient, brothers and sisters,
    until the coming of the Lord.*
*See how the farmer waits for the precious fruit
    of the earth,
      being patient with it
      until it receives the early and the late rains.*
You too must be patient.
*Make your hearts firm,
    because the coming of the Lord is at hand.*

—James 5:7-8

Introduction

Well over a century ago, the German theologian Christoph Freidrich Blumhard observed, "We who are here have been led in a special way to keep what is coming in our hearts and to shape ourselves according to it. That which comes from God—that is what moves our hearts, not only in these days but at all times. That which is to come from God is the most important thing we have, in the past and in the present and in the future."

Advent is a season of promise that challenges us to look to the future, both the near future, when we will recall the Incarnation of Christ at Christmas, and to the end of time, when Christ will return in glory. To say it another way, Advent is a time in the Church's calendar of feasts and seasons that is as much concerned about the future as it is the past.

As Christians, we don't simply believe that the Incarnation—the mystery of God becoming a human being—is a point that can be defined on a calendar or timeline. Instead, because of the great gift given to humanity in the birth of Jesus of Nazareth more than two millennia ago, all of history and what it means to be human has been forever changed.

Through the centuries, great Christian thinkers have struggled to find ways to put this mystery into everyday language. Saint Athanasius of Alexandria wrote, "By taking our nature and offering it in sacrifice, the Word was to destroy it completely and then invest it with His own nature." Saint Maximus "the Confessor" had a slightly different perspective: "The Word of God, born once in the flesh, is always willing to be born spiritually into those who desire Him." I feel, however, that the words of Saint Proclus of Constantinople best sum up the Incarnation and the wonders that are at the heart of Advent and Christmas: "Christ appeared in the world, and bringing beauty out of disarray, gave it luster and joy… *Into the fabric of miracles he interwove ever greater miracles.*"

The four-week season of Advent is a time of miracles. These days have the power to transform us, if we can be open to the graces of the season. Through watching, waiting, silence, and prayer we can begin to recognize all the ways that the Incarnation continues to shape us, our Church, and all of creation. We Christians are an "advent people" who believe that while Christ was born for and among humanity so long ago, we also believe that he comes to us today in word and sacrament and in others. Finally, we believe that he will come again, in glory, in the fullness of time.

In this little book, we will watch and wait for Christ's comings with the saints. These blessed souls lived in the reality of Advent each day of their lives. Worshipping the one who had already come, they sought out and served the Christ who was really present in every person they encountered, and they lived in the constant hope that everything promised to humankind would be fulfilled in the Kingdom of God.

The following reflections and prayers are inspired by the passages of Scripture read during the Mass each day of Advent. The saints, whose lives form an important part of these musings, embodied so many of the Advent virtues. My hope is that their stories will serve as living icons for the promises and prophecies that make up our Church's Advent prayer.

A special feature of the Season of Advent is the days from December 17-23. Unlike the rest of the days of Advent (which can occur on different dates each year), these final days before Christmas are among the most sacred of the Church Year (similar, in fact, to the days of Holy Week). On these days, the theme of Advent shifts to help us prepare to celebrate the mystery of the Nativity at Christmas. This book follows the flow of the liturgy and so, when December 17 arrives, I encourage you begin reading the appropriate reflections for each day.

In structuring this book, I have also included special reflections for three non-Advent celebrations that occur within Advent: the Feast of Saint Andrew the Apostle (November 30), the Solemnity of the Immaculate

Conception (December 8), and the Feast of Our Lady of Guadalupe (December 12). These are major celebrations in the life of the Church and it is most fitting if the reflections for those days are read in place of the Advent reflection. Those three additional reflections are found in the appendix at the end of this book.

The readings for the Mass of each day of Advent have been listed at the end of each day's reflection. If time allows, spend a few moments each day reading these verses, as a way to help focus your attention during what is for many of us the busiest time of the year. Finally, a prayer has been designated for the first three weeks of Advent and for the days of the "O" Antiphons (December 17-23). I want to offer a special word of thanks to Father Harry Hagan, O.S.B., a scripture scholar whose numerous poems and hymn texts have enriched the minds and hearts of so many in the United States and England, myself included. Consider concluding your time of reflection by offering these prayers.

My hope is that this book will help you celebrate Advent with a renewed mind and heart as you journey toward Bethlehem and, ultimately, the Kingdom of God with the saints, whose lives, like the lights of so many stars in a dark sky, help dispel the darkness as we watch and wait for the coming of the Light.

Silas S. Henderson

Foreword

In a retreat conference entitled "The Communion of Saints," Evelyn Underhill, an influential spiritual writer, reminded the retreatants (and us) that our Christian religion has both a visible and invisible side. We are the visible side; the saints are the invisible side. Our faith confirms that there is great mutuality and reciprocity between the two sides. The saints continue to influence our lives in a variety of ways through their writings, their prayers of intercession, and their great witness of holiness.

In Pope Paul VI's *Evangelii Nuntiandi*, one of the greatest pastoral documents of the Church, the Holy Father also reminds us of the importance of the saints. They have been and continue to be mentors and models, teachers and witnesses of our faith life.

Every generation needs to hear about who the saints are and what contributions they have made to furthering God's Kingdom. Silas Henderson continues that tradition in this volume. For some readers, these reflections will be an introduction to one of those mature spiritual personalities (i.e. "saints") who said "yes" to the Lord. For other readers, it will be a reminder of a saint or two who again needs to be heard from and dialogued with.

Come Christmas, we will be better prepared to celebrate the Lord's Nativity because we have spent quality time reflecting upon the lives of the saints and conversing with them. Many of the saints teach us the importance of balance in our spiritual life: balance of prayer and spiritual reading, balance between rest and work, balance between fasting and feasting. The saints demonstrate that the spiritual journey is one of dying to self and consecrating our lives to God's will. The saints witness to the joy of the Gospel and the peace that only the Holy Spirit can give.

Evelyn Underhill shared another insight in her retreat conference: "Through you, God found me." Through the lives and writings of the saints, God often finds us. That is what happened to Saint Augustine who, in reading the life of Saint Anthony of Egypt, resolved to change his life and follow Christ. Perhaps in studying the lives of the saints ("through them"), God will find us out in ever deeper ways.

—Bishop Robert Morneau,
Auxiliary Bishop-Emeritus of Grand Rapids

The First Week of Advent

Prayer

Lord Jesus Christ,
you will come in glory at the end of time
and you come even now in the busy minutes
and in the long hours of our lives.
Teach us how to wait and to trust.

Open our hearts to hear
your promise of mercy and peace
so that, renewed by the faith given to us
and filled with your healing compassion,
we may seek you, our only Light,
and with you shine clearly
in the darkness of sin and death.

We ask this in your name
who are Lord forever and ever. Amen.

—Fr. Harry Hagan, O.S.B.

The First Sunday of Advent

Prepare the way of the Lord, make straight his paths;
All flesh shall see the salvation of God.
　　—Gospel Verse for the First Sunday of Advent

⚜

Although, as the classic holiday song by Meredith Wilson merrily observes, "It's beginning to look a lot like Christmas," it is the call to "vigilant waiting" that best summarizes the message of this first Sunday of Advent. The readings and other texts for today's liturgy all focus on the mystery of the Lord's coming at the end of time.

We should recall, however, that Advent is, above all, a time of hope. While Jesus declares that those who resist him will experience "dismay" and be "perplexed," he also invites those who believe in him to "stand erect and raise your heads because your redemption is at hand" (Luke 21:25-28).

During this month-long season, we prepare to celebrate the Incarnation (the mystery of the Word made flesh) at Christmas and, yet, the

Church also invites us to look toward the future, to the time of the second Advent, when the promise made to the prophets is fulfilled (cf. Jeremiah 33:14). Truly, we live in a time between the comings, the advents, of Christ. As the essayist William Stringfellow reflected, "In the first Advent, Christ came into the world, bringing the good news of salvation; in the next Advent, Christ the Lord comes as Judge of the world, to establish the reign of the Word of God. This is the truth, which the world hates, which we bear in our minds and hearts and by which we live in the world in the time between the two Advents."[1]

Living in the tension of the "time between" is about learning to wait, about not knowing exactly what will come tomorrow and recognizing that, whatever it is, it is part of the mystery of our salvation. Sister Joan Chittister, O.S.B., summarizes it beautifully, when she writes: "The function of Advent is to remind us what we're waiting for as we go through life too busy with things that do not matter to remember the things that do. When year after year we hear the same scripture and the same hymns of longing for the life to come, of which this one is only a shadow, it becomes impossible to forget the refrains of the soul."[2]

Readings:

Year A:

Isaiah 2:1-5 • Romans 13:11-14 • Matthew 24:37-44

Year B:

Isaiah 63:16b-17, 19b; 64:2-7 • 1 Corinthians 1:3-9 • Mark 13:33-37

Year C:

Jeremiah 33:14-16 • 1 Thessalonians 3:12-4:2 • Luke 21:25-28, 34-36

Monday of the First Week of Advent
Saint Francis Xavier

Many will come from the east and west,
and will recline with Abraham, Isaac, and Jacob
at the banquet of the Kingdom of Heaven.
—Matthew 8:11

In the First Reading and Gospel of today's Mass, we hear, as if for the first time, the promise of the Lord's Advent: "For over all, the Lord's glory will be a shelter and protection." The promised Messiah, the Long-Awaited One of Israel, comes to offer salvation for all God's children. Isaiah saw the vision of a world cleansed from its fear and sin, a world where God's glory would be manifest to all. In Jesus, this promise is fulfilled.

Opening our hearts to hear this promise in a new way this Advent, we remember the great missionary, Saint Francis Xavier. Inspired by no other motive than a desire to spread the Gospel, this holy, simple priest left the security of his Jesuit community to set out on a mission that took him to India, numerous islands in the South Pacific, Japan, and finally, to a small island off the coast of China where he died alone, watching and waiting for the Lord he had loved so much.

Enflamed with a desire to see the Good News of the Lord's Coming proclaimed in a new land, Francis Xavier recognized his responsibility to evangelize and share the light of faith.

On this first Monday of Advent, pray that the Holy Spirit will renew the flame of faith within your heart, so that you, like this missionary-priest, may be generous enough to pass along the light of faith that has been entrusted to you.

Readings:
Isaiah 2:1-5 or Isaiah 4:2-6 • Matthew 8:5-11

Tuesday of the First Week of Advent
Saint Dominic Savio

I give you praise, Father, Lord of heaven and earth,
for although you have hidden these things
from the wise and the learned,
you have revealed them to the childlike.

—Luke 10:21

In Isaiah's beloved vision of the peace and concord that will reign on the earth at the Lord's coming, we hear the promise: "The wolf shall be a guest of the lamb, and the leopard shall lie down with the kid; the calf and the young lion shall browse together, with a little child to guide them."

The Readings today challenge us to look for the coming of that Child of the Promise who will bring peace, harmony, and justice to a world torn apart by war, injustice, discrimination, and fear. Children, in their innocence and purity, are free from the cynicism that clouds the vision of so many of us "grown ups," preventing us from seeing what it was that Isaiah saw. The world's little ones—children and those who are children at heart—have the freedom to believe that Isaiah's hope-filled vision can be realized, even in our imperfect world.

When Dominic Savio was born to an impoverished Italian family in 1842, no one could have possibly foreseen how special the boy would be. Although he was only 14 years old when he died in 1857, few would share his clarity of vision and strong faith. It took another saint, his teacher and mentor, John Bosco, to see the promise, the possibility that lay in the child's heart and soul.

Take some time today to reflect on those things in your life that prevent you from trusting in the promises of Advent, especially the promise that the One for whom we are waiting will be and *is being* born in and for you.

Readings:
Isaiah 11:1-10 • Luke 10:21-24

Wednesday of the First Week of Advent
Saint Edmund Campion

My heart is moved with pity for the crowd,
for they have been with me now for three days
and have nothing to eat.
I do not want to send them away hungry,
for fear they will collapse on the way.

—Matthew 15:32

For many in our world, this Advent season will go by unnoticed; even Christmas will be little more than another day. The cold of winter, the gnawing pangs of hunger, the stress of the holiday season, and the insecurities of an unstable economy are all realities of Advent. The pressures of day-to-day life can eclipse the promise that Advent brings to a tired world. It is only by the grace of God that any of us are able to endure the trials and challenges of life in a world where many fight to survive.

For Catholics in England living during the reign of Queen Elizabeth I, the world seemed as though it had been turned upside-down. The

"Old Religion" had been outlawed in favor of the government-sanctioned church. Charges of treason, and even death, awaited those who spoke out against the changes imposed by the queen and her counselors. For those who remained faithful, the sense that they had been abandoned was quite real. It was to this England that the Jesuit priest Edmund Campion returned, prepared to nourish the hungry with the Eucharist and the Word of God. Father Campion, and many others like him, gave their lives to ensure that none of the Lord's hungry children would go without. Although the results of his labors are known only to God, we can look to Saint Edmund as a model of self-sacrifice for the service of those in need.

Advent is a time of patience and of perseverance. Those we honor as saints are Christian women, men, and children who put their faith and devotion first, regardless of whatever challenges and trials they faced. It was the dedication of the saints that kept alive the faith that has been handed down to us. Pray for the grace of perseverance during these dark Advent days.

Readings:
Isaiah 25:6-10a • Matthew 15:29-37

Thursday of the First Week of Advent
Saint Benedict of Nursia

Everyone who listens to these words of mine and
   acts on them
will be like a wise man who built his house on rock.
                                        —Matthew 7:24

※

In a sermon on the text of today's Gospel, the great Syrian bishop Philoxenus of Mabbug reflects, "This saying of our Master obliges us to be diligent in hearing God's word, but also in doing it… God's disciples need to have firmly anchored in their souls the remembrance of their Master, Jesus Christ, and to think of him day and night."[3]

The "Patriarch of Western Monks," Saint Benedict of Nursia, understood that the Christian life begins with a willingness to listen. This is so important to Benedict's view of the spiritual life, that it is the first word of his *Rule*, a document that has guided the lives of Benedictine monks, nuns, and sisters for 1,500 years. Saint Benedict says, "Let us arise, then, at last, for the Scripture stirs us up, saying, 'Now is the hour for us to rise from sleep' (Romans 13:11). Let us open our eyes to the deifying light, let us hear with attentive ears the warning which the divine voice cries daily to us, 'Today if you hear His voice, harden not your hearts' (Psalms 94[95]:8)."[4]

Because Advent is a time of promise, a listening spirit is essential for living the mystery of Advent. The challenge of this season, however, is to discern the call of the Lord's herald who proclaims a message of hope: "Trust in the Lord forever! For the Lord is an eternal Rock" (Isaiah 26:4).

Readings:
Isaiah 26:1-6 • Matthew 7:21, 24-27

Friday of the First Week of Advent
Saint Odilia of Alsace

On that day the deaf shall hear
the words of a book;
And out of gloom and darkness,
the eyes of the blind shall see.
The lowly will ever find joy in the LORD,
and the poor rejoice in the Holy One of Israel.
                                        —Isaiah 29:18-19

❧

In reflecting on the light of the Lord that illumines the darkened heart of the sinful person, Quaker writer Isaac Pennington wrote, "But of what nature is this light, which shineth in man in his dark state? It is of a living nature; it is light which flows from life; it is light which hath life in it; it is the life of our Lord Jesus Christ, of the Word eternal, which is the light of men."[5] Pennington recognized that it is only the Light of the World who can drive away the darkness of sin and death which seeks to cover the earth with its heavy pall.

And yet, Isaiah the prophet understood the Advent of the Promised One would bring light where there was once darkness and unstop that which was once closed. The wonder that Jesus performed when he gave sight to the blind men is a confirmation that it was he of whom Isaiah spoke.

The gift of sight, unobscured by sin, despair, and doubt, is truly a grace and allows the Christian to view the world with the eyes of faith. Saint Odilia, who lived in the Alsace region of France, knew the true value of the gift of sight—both physical and spiritual sight. Born blind and rejected by her father because of her physical limitation, she lived in darkness and isolation until she was given the gift of sight and a name (Odilia is a form of *Sol Dei*, "God's light") at the time of her baptism. Saint Odilia later became a highly regarded abbess who dedicated her life to the care of the nuns of her community and to works of mercy, feeding the hungry and caring for the sick and pilgrims— the poor in whom she saw the presence of Christ. Today, Saint Odilia (along with Saint Lucy) is honored as a patron saint of the blind.

Advent is a season of darkness, a time of watching and waiting for the coming of the Light of the

World. It is faith which enables us to recognize that God's Providence is at work, even though events in our world and our individual lives may make us feel that there is only darkness around us. The faith of the two blind men healed in today's Gospel and of the saints—like the once-blind Saint Odilia—remind us that if our faith is strong, we will never be disappointed in our waiting (cf. Psalm 27:13-14): "Behold, our Lord shall come with power; he will enlighten the eyes of his servants" (Alleluia Verse).

Today, pray for greater faith in the One who is the Light of the World.

Readings:
Isaiah 29:17-24 • Matthew 9:27-31

Saturday of the First Week of Advent
Saints Frances Cabrini, Theodora Guerin, Rose Philippine Duchesne, and Marianne Cope

At the sight of the crowds,
Jesus' heart was moved with pity for them
because they were troubled and abandoned...
Then he said to his disciples,
"The harvest is abundant but the laborers are few;
so ask the master of the harvest
to send out laborers for the harvest."

—Matthew 9:36-38

Compassion is not a uniquely Christian virtue, but it is a spirit of empathy for the suffering of others that is a fundamental part of how we Christians are to love. Ultimately, to have compassion isn't just about being kind; rather, it means to share in the sufferings of another person. Pope Benedict XVI reflected that the mandate to love one another demands that we "acknowledge our responsibility towards those who, like ourselves, are creatures and children of

God…If we cultivate this way of seeing others as our brothers and sisters, solidarity, justice, mercy and compassion will naturally well up in our hearts" (*Message for Lent*, 2011).

Women religious have always stood with those on the margins of society and Saints Frances Xavier Cabrini, Theodora Guerin, Rose Philippine Duchesne, and Marianne Cope—women religious who served in the American missions—were certainly no exceptions. These women left their homes and the security of their religious communities and worked as missionaries, seeking out and serving immigrants, the uneducated, the sick and dying, and the poor. They spread the Gospel through compassionate care of those God called them to serve, bringing the healing presence of Christ—without cost they had received, without cost they gave all they had (cf. Matthew 10:8).

This Advent, watching for the presence of the Lord among us, we also recall that our compassion for others is a sign of God's compassion, of the coming of the One who brings comfort and healing in his wings (cf. Malachi 4:2).

Readings:
Isaiah 30:19-21, 23-26 • Matthew 9:25-10:1, 5-8

The Second Week of Advent

Prayer

Called by John the Baptist to prepare the way,
we ask, Lord our God,
for courage and perseverance
to live in the present of this moment
and to be more and different
than we had thought or hoped.

As Christ, the Good Shepherd,
became flesh among us,
may we, by your mercy and grace,
become Christ to all in need,
and so proclaim the Gospel
in all that we say and do.

Grant this through Jesus who comes
even this day in glory. Amen.

—*Fr. Harry Hagan, O.S.B.*

The Second Sunday of Advent

Prepare the way of the Lord, make straight his paths;
All flesh shall see the salvation of God.
　—Gospel Verse for the Second Sunday of Advent

❧

W e live in an age of sound bites and blogs, in a world of competing viewpoints and voices. It can sometimes be difficult to discern what is really worthy of our attention. While we may not often think of it in this way, Advent is a season of discernment. As one of the Readings of Scripture assigned to this Sunday reminds us, it was to this spirit of discernment that St. Paul called the Philippians when he wrote, "this is my prayer: that your love may increase ever more and more in knowledge and every kind of perception, to discern what is of value, so that you may be pure and blameless for the day of Christ" (1:9-10).

If we settle for the mediocrity of sound bites and half-truths, without seeking to discern what is truly important, we run the risk of losing sight of the hopes and promises that can only find fulfillment in a life commitment to Christ.

The prophecies of Isaiah and Baruch and the call of John the Baptist that we hear on the Second Sunday of Advent remind us of what it is we are called to be and do. In essence, John the Baptist's call to "prepare the way for the Lord" is a charge to discern the voice of the Lord calling out to us and to persevere in the way of faith. The priest and theologian Origen helps us to understand what this means for us today: "Is it not a way within ourselves that we have to prepare for the Lord? Is it not a straight and level highway in our hearts that we are to make ready? Surely this is the way by which the Word of God enters… Prepare a way for the Lord by living a good life and guard that way by good works. Let the Word of God move in you unhindered and give you a knowledge of his coming and of his mysteries" (*Homilies on Luke*, 21).

Readings:

Year A:
Isaiah 11:1-10 • Romans 15:4-9 • Matthew 3:1-12

Year B:
Isaiah 40:1-5, 9-11 • 2 Peter 3:8-14 • Mark 1:1-8

Year C:
Baruch 5:1-9 • Philippians 1:4-6, 8-11 • Luke 3:1-6

Monday of the Second Week of Advent
Saint Peter Claver

Strengthen the hands that are feeble,
make firm the knees that are weak,
Say to those whose hearts are frightened:
Be strong, fear not!

—Isaiah 35:3-4

Throughout his Gospel, the evangelist Luke consistently reminds us of the special care and concern that Jesus showed for the poor, the outcast, and the sinner. The healing of the paralytic, only one of the many acts of healing related by Saint Luke, was a sign that the promise made through the prophet Isaiah would be fulfilled: The coming of the Lord would be a time of healing and renewal for Israel and an exiled people would be given a home forever: "Those whom the LORD has ransomed will return and enter Zion singing, crowned with everlasting joy; They will meet with joy and gladness, sorrow and mourning will flee" (Isaiah 35:10).

Saint Peter Claver, a 17th century Jesuit missionary who served in Colombia, dedicated his life to serving enslaved Africans brought to the New World amid the most horrific and inhuman circumstances. This priest, who called himself the "slave of the slaves," boarded the slave ships as soon as they came into port, tending to the sickest and dying slaves first. After the slaves were herded into pens, he remained with them, distributing medicine, food, and other goods, encouraging them, teaching them that they were loved by God, and telling them about Jesus. Although it is said that Peter Claver baptized more than 300,000 slaves, his ministry also extended to the plantations and farms where he fought for the civil and religious rights of the slaves.

The spirit of generosity and hope of Advent calls for a renewed commitment to share our blessings with those who are poor and abandoned: "Near indeed is his salvation to those who fear him, glory dwelling in our land" (Psalm 85:10).

Readings:
Isaiah 35:1-10 • Luke 5:17-26

Tuesday of the Second Week of Advent
Blessed Charles de Foucauld

*If a man has a hundred sheep and one of them
    goes astray,
will he not leave the ninety-nine in the hills
and go in search of the stray?...*

*In just the same way, it is not the will of your
    heavenly Father
that one of these little ones be lost.*

—Matthew 18:12, 14

The image of the Good Shepherd is one of the most well-beloved ways of understanding God's provident care. Saint Gregory the Great, reflecting on Christ, the Good Shepherd, noted that anyone who follows this Shepherd will "enter into a life of faith; from faith he will go out to vision, from belief to contemplation, and will graze in the good pastures of everlasting life… Beloved, let us set out for these pastures, where we shall keep joyful festival with so many of our fellow citizens." He concluded, "No matter what obstacles we encounter, we must not allow them to turn us aside from the joy of the heavenly feast" (*Homily 14*, 3-6).

For the exiled people of Israel, this vision of the One who would tend the flock and gather the lambs into his arms (cf. Isaiah 40:11) was a foreshadowing of that Good Shepherd who would gather the Church from among the nations.

No one who knew Charles de Foucauld as a young man would probably ever imagine that he would not only come to dedicate his life to this Good Shepherd, but that he would, himself, become a pastor to the nomadic Tuareg people of Algeria's Sahara Desert. A new kind of missionary, he left behind the wealth of his childhood and the security of his Trappist monastery to live among the poorest people in the world, sharing their life and hardships. He wrote: "In order to save us, God came to us and lived among us, from the Annunciation to the Ascension, in a close and familiar way. God continues to come to us and to live with us in a close and familiar way, each day and at every hour, in the holy Eucharist. So we too must go and live among our brothers and sisters in a close and familiar way."

Charles' contemplative heart and generous spirit allowed him to truly understand the meaning of the Incarnation—that God had come among men and women, to share in and redeem the struggles of humanity. He modeled his life after the example of Jesus who is Emmanuel, "God With Us."

Readings:
Isaiah 40:1-11 • Matthew 18:12-14

Wednesday of the Second Week of Advent
Saint Josephine Bakhita

Jesus said to the crowds:
"Come to me, all you who labor and are burdened,
And I will give you rest.
Take my yoke upon you and learn from me,
For I am meek and humble of heart;
And you will find rest for yourselves.
For my yoke is easy, and my burden light."
—Matthew 11:28-30

The words of Jesus are not simply idle, poetic phrases. Jesus addresses real human experiences of fatigue, despair, downheartedness, and even exploitation and abuse. Just as the Lord does not "faint or grow weary" in protecting the Chosen People, he gives strength and vigor to the fainting and weak, so that "they who hope in the Lord will renew their strength, they will soar as with eagles' wings; They will run and not grow weary, walk and not grow faint" (Isaiah 40:30-31).

To live a life faithful to the demands of the Gospel requires conviction and strength that can waiver, no matter how good and pure our intentions may be. Jesus' words are addressed to each of us: in the moments when we are tempted to stray from the way to which we have committed ourselves, these words should offer us comfort. He is with us, sharing the burden. As Saint Bruno of Segni reflected, "Although he was the almighty Lord, he chose to be poor for our sakes, he refused honors, freely submitted to sufferings… and he did all this in order that we might not disdain to follow him insofar as our frailty allows" (*Sermon I on Good Friday*).

Saint Josephine Bakhita was kidnapped in her native Sudan and sold into slavery when she was only nine years old. The trauma of her abduction and enslavement was so severe that she actually forgot her own name; the name by which she was known, "Bakhita," was an Arabic word meaning "lucky." Ultimately, after being purchased by an Italian family, she was introduced to the Christian Faith and, after gaining her freedom, she became a religious sister in Italy. She exclaimed, "I am definitively loved and whatever happens to me— I am awaited by this Love." She found true freedom in following the God who had suffered so much for her (cf. Romans 8:21).

Josephine Bakhita spent her freedom in service to others, stressing the truth of God's loving care to all those whom she encountered. In his encyclical, *Saved In Hope*, Pope Benedict XVI celebrated this holy woman, as he observed, "The liberation she had received through her encounter with the God of Jesus Christ, she felt she had to extend, it had to be handed on to others, to the greatest possible number of people. The hope born in her which had 'redeemed' her she could not keep to herself; this hope had to reach many, to reach everybody" (3).

As we continue our Advent watching, pray for the gifts of courage and perseverance. And remember, the night is always darkest just before the coming of the dawn: "The sky will clear. And in the night, you will see a star shining in the dark... There is hope. Love never dies... Just as surely as day follows night, a new dawn awaits you."[6]

Readings:
Isaiah 40:25-31 • Matthew 11:28-30

Thursday of the Second Week of Advent
Saint Maximilian Kolbe

I will set in the wasteland the cypress,
together with the plane tree and the pine,
That all may see and know,
observe and understand,
That the hand of the Lord has done this,
the Holy One of Israel has created it.

—Isaiah 41:19b-20

❦

Advent is a season of tension. It is a time to reflect on promises fulfilled, but somehow still incomplete. This built-in tension of Advent reflects the experience of waiting and expectation that is an essential part of life. When we think of a child counting the days until Christmas or listen to the hopes and excitement of parents awaiting the birth of a child, we can see the frustration (and even pain) that goes with expectation. Unfortunately, however, many people today live lives that are almost always oriented toward the next thing: we love novelty and distractions so much that we often forget about the gift of the present moment. Advent isn't only about the past and the future, it is also a season that invites us to see what God is doing at this moment.

If we spend our lives always looking into some far-distant future, always scanning the horizon for signs and wonders, then we can miss the miracles of the present moment. More often than we think, God comes to us in the people and things of our lives and this is all part of the recreation of the world that is an essential part of the promise of Advent.

When Saint Maximilian Kolbe, a Polish Franciscan imprisoned in the concentration camp at Auschwitz because of his opposition to Nazism, offered to die in place of a condemned husband and father, he recognized that God was calling him to make the most of that moment—a moment to be Christ for another person that would never come again.

The *Communion Antiphon* for the Mass of Thursday of the Second Week of Advent reminds us: "Let us live justly and devoutly in this age, as we await the blessed hope, and the coming of the glory of our great God" (cf. Titus 2:12-13).

Wait. Live in the tension of Advent.
Watch. Because he is coming to you today.

Readings:
Isaiah 41:13-20 • Matthew 11:11-15

Friday of the Second Week of Advent
Saint Francis of Assisi

Jesus said to the crowds:
"The Son of Man came eating and drinking and
*   they said,*
'Look, he is a glutton and a drunkard,
a friend of tax collectors and sinners.'
But wisdom is vindicated by her works."
                                    —Matthew 11:18-19

❧

There is a sad irony that those who longed for the coming of the Messiah were not able to recognize his presence among them for the simple reason that he did not come in the way they expected. And yet, as Blessed William of Saint-Thierry observed, everything Jesus did and said on earth, "even enduring insults, the spitting, the buffeting—the cross and the grave—all of this was actually [the Father] speaking to us in the Son, appealing to us by love."[7]

There are, in Christian tradition, saints who are known as "Holy Fools." These are men and women who rejected the world's values and followed Christ in a dynamic way, living out the words of Saint Paul: "We are fools on Christ's account... To this very hour we go hungry and thirsty, we are poorly clad and roughly treated, we wander about homeless" (1 Corinthians 4:10a, 11). Old Testament figures such as Isaiah and Hosea and saints like Alexius of Rome and Benedict Joseph Labre all embody this spirit.

Perhaps the best-known "Holy Fool" in the west is Saint Francis of Assisi. When Francis dramatically stripped himself in the town square in Assisi, taking "Lady Poverty" as his bride, he committed himself to living out the Gospel in a radical way. But, like Jesus, he was condemned by those who had no use for his prophetic witness. Francis understood that God's Wisdom, perfectly embodied in the mystery of the God-made-man, surpasses our limited understanding: "I the LORD, your God, teach you what is for your good, and lead you on the way you should go" (Isaiah 48:17).

Readings:
Isaiah 48:17-19 • Matthew 11:16-19

Saturday of the Second Week of Advent
Saint Thomas More

In those days,
like a fire there appeared the prophet Elijah
whose words were as a flaming furnace.
Their staff of bread he shattered,
in his zeal he reduced them to straits;
By the Lord's word he shut up the heavens
and three times brought down fire.
How awesome are you, Elijah, in your
     wondrous deeds!

—*Sirach 28:1-4*

I n the Advent carol "Watchman Tell Us of the Night," the lyricist, Sir John Bowring, presents a dialogue between a watchman and a traveler. In the song, the night is far spent and the morning star announces the coming of the dawn:

> *Watchman, tell us of the night,*
> *What its signs of promise are.*

Traveler, o'er yon mountains height,
See that glory beaming star.
Watchman, does its beauteous ray
Aught of joy or hope foretell?
Traveler, yes—it brings the day,
Promised day of Israel.

A prophet, like the watchman in this carol, is the one who is able to discern the presence and action of God at work in the world and who is sent to communicate God's will for the world. Advent is a season of prophets: Elijah, Baruch, Micah, Zechariah, among others, and, most especially, Isaiah, and John the Baptist.

The call to serve as a prophet was not limited to figures in Sacred Scripture. Throughout the history of the Church, men and women have engaged the world around them, admonishing, challenging, inspiring, and changing the lives of those whom they encountered, giving voice to God's presence and desires for every person.

When Saint Thomas More refused to submit to King Henry VIII's demand that More recognize him as supreme head of the Church in England, he became part of the long procession of prophets who wind their way through history. The Second

Vatican Council reminded us that all Christians share in the prophetic mission of Jesus, himself (see *Lumen Gentium*, 12). Saint John Paul II elaborated on this by reminding all Christians that we have the "ability and responsibility to accept the gospel in faith and to proclaim it in word and deed, without hesitating to courageously identify and denounce evil… to allow the newness and the power of the gospel to shine out every day" (*Christifideles laici*, 14).

As we look forward to the Third Sunday of Advent, reflect on how you can joyfully live out the prophetic message that has been entrusted to you, personally and individually.

Readings:
Sirach 48:1-4, 9-11 • Matthew 17:9a, 10-13

The Third Week of Advent

Prayer

Teach us, Lord Jesus Christ, to rejoice.
Teach us to rejoice in your Cross
and to find the joy of the Holy Spirit
in the brokenness of this world.

In this season of mercy,
touch our heart with your heart
move us with your compassionate love
so that we may rejoice in our vocation as
    Christians
and so bring healing and wholeness,
comfort and peace to this world.

We ask this in your Name
who are Lord forever and ever. Amen.

—Fr. Harry Hagan, O.S.B.

The Third Sunday of Advent

Rejoice in the Lord always; again I say, rejoice.
Indeed, the Lord is near.

—Entrance Antiphon for
the Third Sunday of Advent

O n this Third Sunday of Advent, the Church gives us a very particular mandate: *Rejoice!* And during these preChristmas days, it seems that there is joy all around us. And yet, the words of the essayist William Stringfellow give us pause: "For the greeting card sentiment and sermonic rhetoric, I do not think that much rejoicing happens around Christmastime, least of all about the coming of the Lord. There is, I notice, a lot of holiday frolicking, but that is not the same as rejoicing. In any case, maybe the outbursts of either frolicking or rejoicing are premature, if John the Baptist has credibility. He identifies *repentance* as the sentiment of Advent."[8]

The themes of judgment, repentance, and salvation which emerge in the Gospels for this Sunday seem to be at odds with the spirit of Christian joy to which we are also called. John the Baptist, the prophet *par excellence*, proclaims the coming of the Christ as he calls his hearers to lead lives worthy of the new age of the Messiah: give up extortion and avarice and begin sharing with those who are in need. In short, manifest your interior faith through works of charity, peace, and justice.

How can we reconcile these seemingly disparate ideas of repentance and joy? In answering this question, we can take a cue from Thomas Merton who observed that the "'King who is to come' is more than a charming smiling infant in the straw… In Advent we celebrate the coming and indeed the presence of Christ in our world. We witness to his presence even in the midst of all its inscrutable problems and tragedies."[9]

What we prepare to commemorate at Christmas has actually happened: God is in our midst. John's clarion call for repentance is an exhortation for us to acknowledge the presence of Christ among us and to live accordingly. And so, our Advent—hope and joy are not only focused on the approach of Christmas Day. Rather, we rejoice because God has kept his promises and has given us love and truth in Jesus.

Readings:

Year A:
Isaiah 35:1-6a, 10 • James 5:7-10 • Matthew 11:2-11

Year B:
Isaiah 61:1-2a, 10-11 • 1 Thessalonians 5:16-24 •
John 1:6-8, 19-28

Year C:
Zephaniah 3:14-18a • Philippians 4:4-7 •
Luke 3:10-18

Monday of the Third Week of Advent
Saint Teresa Benedicta of the Cross

The utterance of one who hears what God says,
and knows what the Most High knows,
of one who sees what the Almighty sees,
enraptured, and with eyes unveiled.
I see him, though not now;
I behold him, though not near:
A star shall advance from Jacob,
and a staff shall rise from Israel.

—Numbers 24:16-17

With today's prophecy from Balaam (Numbers 24:15-17a), a non-Israelite prophet, our attention is drawn more and more to who Jesus is: the star rising from Jacob and the staff for Israel (cf. Isaiah 11:1).

Even a brief reading of the Old Testament will reveal that the people of Israel were a hope-filled, expectant people. Israel's longing for the Messiah was shaped by the ways that God had manifested his power throughout their history. And prophets like Isaiah, Amos, and later, John the Baptist never stopped reminding the people that God was coming to save his own. But, Israel also recognized that God had already shown his power and "visited his people." The God of Israel was a God who was always with them, ready to support and protect them.

It was from this waiting people that the German-born Jewish philosopher, Edith Stein, was born. Like her ancestors, she was a seeker. Although she rejected her Jewish heritage as a young woman, her search for truth ultimately led her to know Christ and to commit herself to him as a Carmelite nun, known as Teresa Benedicta of the Cross.

Acutely aware of the sufferings of the Jewish people during World War II, she willingly accepted their common fate, seeing that Christ's cross redeemed all aspects of life, even the horrendous violence perpetrated against her people: "To suffer and to be happy although suffering, to have one's feet on the earth, to walk in the dirty and rough paths of this earth and yet to be enthroned with Christ at the Father's right hand, to laugh and cry with the children of this world and ceaselessly sing the praises of God with the choirs of angels—

this is the life of the Christian until the morning of eternity breaks forth."[10]

As we continue Advent, take time today to reflect on the ways God has revealed himself in your life—both in his power and in the whispers of your heart.

Readings:
Numbers 24:2-7, 15-17a • Matthew 21:23-27

Tuesday of the Third Week of Advent
Saint Mary of Egypt

The LORD is close to the brokenhearted;
and those who are crushed in spirit he saves.
The LORD redeems the lives of his servants;
no one incurs guilt who takes refuge in him.
—Psalm 34:19, 23

S acred Scripture reminds us that God
"knows how we were formed; that we were
made of dust" (Psalm 103:14). These simple,
unsophisticated words are in fact a profound
statement of faith. They acknowledge that all that
we have and are is a gift of God. Beyond this, we
are also reminded that we are all made of the
same "stuff"—we are all capable of every sinful
act the human mind can imagine. Our shared,
broken human nature is the great equalizer.

Mercy is that compassion or forgiveness that is
shown toward someone, even when it is within
one's power to punish or harm the offender. To
say that God is all-merciful is to acknowledge that

God also has absolute power. For our part, we show mercy because we remember that we are like other people.

Many of us have a stereotype of saints that make them larger-than-life figures possessing an extraordinary holiness that is so far removed from our experience that they become irrelevant. And yet, in reading their lives and writings, we quickly discover that the saints recognized their need for God's mercy much more readily than many of us in our most contrite moments.

For Saint Mary of Egypt, God's mercy became the sole focus of her life. After undergoing a profound conversion, abandoning life as a prostitute after being moved by an icon of the Mother of God holding her infant Son, her entire life became one long vigil, wandering in the desert, "looking for the Lord who saves the poor."[11]

We don't often think of Advent as a season of mercy. But, as we look forward to celebrating the coming of Christ in history, mystery, and majesty during the Christmas Season, we have these days to prepare.

Don't spend these final days of Advent passively, allowing time to pass while we wait for Christmas. Make the most of the time we have by seeking reconciliation for yourself and offering forgiveness to those who need your mercy and compassion.

Readings:
Zephaniah 3:1-2, 9-13 • Matthew 21:28-32

Wednesday of the Third Week of Advent
Saint Alphonsus Liguori

Jesus said to them,
"Go and tell John what you have seen and heard:
the blind regain their sight,
the lame walk;
lepers are cleansed,
the deaf hear, the dead are raised,
the poor have the good news proclaimed to them."
—Luke 7:22

The question of who Jesus was posed challenges not only for John the Baptist, but for the early Church as well. Even the briefest surveys of Church history reveal dozens of theological debates, intrigues, and heresies over Christ's divinity and humanity, what his death really meant, and how he lives in the Church today. And yet, this passage from the Gospel of Luke, offered in answer to John's question, reveals that Jesus was and is the One who will fulfill all our hopes and who offers the healing and wholeness our broken world needs so badly.

For centuries, heroic men and women have proclaimed the Good News of God's Kingdom to the poor. The call to evangelize isn't limited to those living as missionaries in exotic parts of the world. Saint John Paul II reflected in his encyclical on the mission of the Church (*Redemptoris Missio*): "The missionary who, despite all his or her human limitations and defects, lives a simple life, taking Christ as the model, is a sign of God and of transcendent realities. But everyone in the Church, striving to imitate the Divine Master, can and must bear this kind of witness; in many cases, it is the only possible way of being a missionary" (42).

Saint Alphonsus Liguori, bishop, theologian, and founder of the Congregation of the Most Holy Redeemer, dedicated his life to proclaiming the Good News to the poor, sending his Redemptorist sons to impoverished, remote areas where the Church had little or no influence. One of the greatest moral theologians in Christian history, he succeeded in his mission because love was his guiding principle: he understood that preaching God's mercy was the essential first step of proclaiming the Gospel effectively. Saint Alphonsus reminds us, "The Son of God made himself little to make us great. He gave himself to us that we might give ourselves to him. He came to show us his love that we might respond to it by giving him ours. Therefore, let us receive him with affection, let us love him and turn to him in all our needs."[12]

Readings:
Isaiah 45:6c-8, 18, 21c-25 • Luke 7:18b-23

Thursday of the Third Week of Advent
Saint Hildegard of Bingen

With enduring love I take pity on you,
*says the L*ORD*, your redeemer…*
Though the mountains leave their place
and the hills be shaken,
my love shall never leave you
nor my covenant of peace be shaken,
*says the L*ORD*, who has mercy on you.*

—Isaiah 54:5, 10

Peace. It is a word emblazoned on Advent banners and printed in delicate gold script on Christmas cards. But do we really understand what the promise of peace means? Rather than simply being the opposite of war, oppression, unrest, or discomfort, peace is, to quote Saint Augustine, "the tranquility of order," or, to say it another way, it is the result of all things being in their proper order and place.[13] The quest for peace is an essential part of the Christian vocation. As Cardinal Basil Hume observed, "Peace is so very precious, but it begins in the human heart… It comes when we want what is right, and strive to achieve what is good… It is the constant attempt to open up our lives to God, and when he invades the human heart, he establishes peace within his newly won kingdom."[14]

Although we can work for peace by promoting the dignity of all people, only Christ can bring us true peace: "He is our peace… He came and preached peace to you who were far and peace to those who were near" (Ephesians 2:14, 17a).

Saint Hildegard of Bingen lived in an age marked by unrest, excess, and renewal. While she joined other religious leaders in working to restore the health of Church, she never lost sight of her primary vocation: to seek God as a Benedictine nun. Taking to heart the words of Saint Benedict, "make peace your quest and your aim," Hildegard sought and achieved interior peace and union with Christ, the Prince of Peace (cf. *Rule of St. Benedict*, Prologue:17). In this way, she obtained the freedom and the clarity of vision to become a champion of peace in her own time and through the centuries.

As we continue to look toward Christmas, take a few quiet moments and reflect on the ways you can promote peace in your own life and in the world around you.

Readings:
Isaiah 54:1-10 • Luke 7:24-30

Friday of the Third Week of Advent
Saint Paul

May God have pity on us and bless us;
may he let his face shine upon us.
So may your way be known upon earth;
among all nations, your salvation.

—Psalm 67:2-3

Saint Peter Chrysologus observed, "Mortal man, enshrouded always in darkness, must not be left in ignorance, and so be deprived of what he can understand and retain only by grace. In choosing to be born for us, God chose to be known by us."[15] The God who created and sustains us wants to be known and loved by his creation. And, as Saint Paul reminds us, Jesus was the perfect revelation of God's love: "He is the image of the invisible God, the firstborn of all creation. For in him were created all things in heaven and on earth, things visible and invisible… For in him all the fullness was pleased to dwell, and through him to reconcile all things for him, making peace by the blood of his cross" (Colossians 1:15,16a, 20a).

It was love for Jesus, who is *Emmanuel: God-With-Us*, that prompted Saint Paul to leave behind the security of the world he knew to risk everything to take the Good News throughout the Mediterranean world.

Paul was keenly aware of the unique role he was being asked to play in the life of the Church. As the "Apostle of the Gentiles," he looked beyond the boundaries of his own nation and faith-heritage and imagined a world renewed and restored by the same Jesus who had so completely changed his life on the road to Damascus. But Saint Paul's conversion and faith wasn't based upon some sort of psychological process or an intellectual awakening. Instead, it was the fruit of his meeting with Jesus. Ultimately, as Pope Benedict XVI has observed, Christianity "is not a new philosophy or a new form of morality. We are only Christians if we encounter Christ, even if He does not reveal Himself to us as clearly and irresistibly as he did to Paul in making the Apostles of the Gentiles." Advent calls us to be aware of the ways we encounter Christ in reading Sacred Scripture, in prayer, and in the liturgical and sacramental life of the Church, to "touch Christ's heart and feel that Christ touches ours. And it is only in this personal relationship with Christ, in this meeting with the Risen One, that we are truly Christian" (*General Audience*, September 3, 2008).

Readings:
Isaiah 56:1-3a, 6-8 • John 5:33-36

The Fourth Week of Advent

Prayer for the Days of the "O" Antiphons and the Fourth Sunday of Advent

O *Wisdom*, you know the human heart,

O *Leader of Ancient Israel*, you come in all humility,

O *Root of Jesse's Stem*, you bring the promise of the Father,

O *Key of David*, you open and no one closes,

O *Radiant Dawn*, you shine on those who walk in darkness,

O *King of All Nations*, you rule in mercy and in love,

O *Emmanuel*, you are God with us and among us:

Draw us to your eternal light
that we may see what you see
and love what you love.
Come! Lord Jesus! Come! Amen.

—*Fr. Harry Hagan, O.S.B.*

The Fourth Sunday of Advent

The virgin shall conceive and bear a son,
And they shall name him Emmanuel.

—Gospel Verse for
the Fourth Sunday of Advent (Year A)

☙

Reflecting on the mystery of the Incarnation, Saint Irenaeus of Lyons wrote that "God is man's glory. Man is the vessel which receives God's action and all his wisdom and power." In these final days of Advent, the Church shifts her focus from the advent of Christ at the end of time, to preparing for Christmas. In a particular way, today we are invited to reflect on Mary, the Mother of Jesus.

In the story of Mary's visit to her elderly kinswoman, Elizabeth, we are presented with two women who are living in expectation. Elizabeth, pregnant with John the Baptist, and Mary, carrying God within her, embody the hopes and expectations of Israel. Theirs was a waiting full of promise: "People who have to wait have received a promise that allows them to wait. They have received something that is at work in them, like a seed that has started to grow."[16] This kind of waiting is never a movement from nothing to something. Rather, it is a movement from something to something more.

In his own time, God had called the patriarchs and prophets, Abraham, Moses, David, Isaiah, Jeremiah, and so many others, to prepare the way for his Son (cf. Hebrews 1:1-2 and *Dei Verbum*, 3). And, in Mary and her Child, the promises, hopes, and expectations of God's own people were finally being fulfilled: "from you shall come forth from me one who is to be ruler in Israel; whose origin is from of old, from ancient times… He shall stand firm and shepherd his flock" (Micah 5:1, 3a).

For centuries, the Ark of the Covenant was a sign of God's commitment and promise to Israel. The Ark was an icon of God's presence, a reminder that God was in their midst, accompanying the people as they wandered through the desert and fought to claim a home and identity (cf. Numbers 10:35-36). Mary became the new tabernacle, the new, living Ark of the Covenant, who carried God within her. In Mary, God was now present in a person, in a heart. And, just as David danced before the Ark of the Lord, John the Baptist, still in Elizabeth's womb, leapt for joy because the Lord had come (2 Samuel 6:14; Luke 1:44).

In these last days of Advent, Mary teaches us how to receive the Word of God, whose coming we celebrate at Christmas. Saint John Paul II observed, "She exhorts us, first of all, to *humility*, so that God can find space in our heart, not darkened by pride or arrogance. She points out to us the value of *silence*, which knows how to listen to the song of the Angels and the crying of the Child, not stifling them by noise and confusion. Together with her, we stop before the Nativity scene with intimate *wonder*, savoring the simple and pure *joy* that this Child gives to humanity" (*Angelus*, December 21, 2003).

Readings:

Year A:
Isaiah 7:10-14 • Romans 1:1-7 • Matthew 1:18-24
Year B:
2 Samuel 7:1-5, 8b-12, 14a, 16 • Romans 16:25-27 • Luke 1:26-38
Year C:
Micah 5:1-4a • Hebrews 10;5-10 • Luke 1:39-45

December 17-23
The Days of the "O Antiphons"

Decmber 17 marks the beginning of the "O" Antiphons, privileged days celebrated the week before Christmas. Following the tradition of the Church, the prayers, Scripture readings, and reflections for these days take the place of the other days of Advent.

An important part of this tradition is the custom of singing the "O" Antiphons. These chants (which are the inspiration for the popular Advent hymn "O Come, O Come Emmanuel") use invocations and titles of Christ drawn from the prophetic and wisdom writings of the Old Testament.

Prayer for the Days of the "O" Antiphons and the Fourth Sunday of Advent

O Wisdom, you know the human heart,
O Leader of Ancient Israel, you come in all
    humility,
O Root of Jesse's Stem, you bring the promise of
    the Father,
O Key of David, you open and no one closes,
O Radiant Dawn, you shine on those who walk
    in darkness,
O King of All Nations, you rule in mercy and in
    love,
O Emmanuel, you are God with us and among us:

Draw us to your eternal light
that we may see what you see
and love what you love.
Come! Lord Jesus! Come! Amen.

                        —*Fr. Harry Hagan, O.S.B.*

December 17 • O Wisdom
Saint Aloysius Gonzaga

He crouches like a lion recumbent,
the king of beasts—who would dare rouse him?
The scepter shall never depart from Judah,
or the mace from between his legs,
While tribute is brought to him,
and he receives the people's homage.

—Genesis 49:9b-10

The entrance of God into the world at the birth of Jesus is an event which forever changed the course of human history. In fact, the Incarnation of Christ is the fulfillment of history. The promises made to the patriarchs and prophets, the hopes of God's chosen people, and the visions of seers and sages from far-away places were realized in the birth of the Christ at Bethlehem.

The power of the new-born King, the One who would rule God's people with justice, and the afflicted with right judgment (cf. Psalm 72:2), found its most perfect expression not in the signs and wonders that Jesus worked, but in his stretching out his hand, granting freedom and absolution to his people, as he hung upon the cross: "He stretched out his hands when he suffered in order to deliver from suffering those who believed in him" (Saint Hippolytus of Rome, *Traditio apostolica*).

Saint Aloysius Gonzaga was the eldest son and heir of one of the most powerful, influential, and, at times, corrupt families in 16th-century Italy. A prince of the Holy Roman Empire, he walked away from wealth and power, his birthright, to enter the Society of Jesus. Far from the safety and privilege of the palaces of his youth, Aloysius died at the age of 23 after carrying to a hospital a plague victim he found lying on a Roman street.

Aloysius knew the importance of family and of family history. He would have recognized his own family story in the genealogy of Jesus—a mix of saints and sinners. The unlikely assortment of the good, bad, and indifferent that makes up Jesus' family tree (proclaimed in today's Gospel) is also a perfect image of the Church. As Gail Godwin observed, "Matthew's genealogy contained—and continues to contain—the flawed and inflicted and insulted, the cunning and the weak-willed and the misunderstood. His are an equal opportunity ministry for crooks and saints."[17] It is a powerful testament, as we enter these days of final preparation for Christmas, that God is using us, with our gifts, talents, flaws, failures, and like Aloysius, family histories, to bring him into the world today.

Readings:
Genesis 49:2, 8-10 • Matthew 1:1-17

December 18 • O Leader of Ancient Israel
Saint Joseph

An angel of the Lord appeared to him
in a dream and said,
"Joseph, son of David,
do not be afraid to take Mary your wife
into your home.
For it is through the Holy Spirit
that this child has been conceived in her."
—Matthew 1:20

In the 15th-century "Cherry Tree Carol," Joseph and Mary are making their way to Bethlehem when, stopping in a cherry orchard, Mary asks Joseph to pick some cherries for her. Joseph, with spite, answers, "Let the father of the baby gather cherries for thee." In the carol, it is only after witnessing a miracle of the cherry tree bending down to offer fruit to Mary that Joseph accepts the divine nature of his young wife's pregnancy.

This song, however, hardly reflects the simple obedience and faith Joseph shows in the Gospel for December 18. Although the gospels do not relate any words of Joseph, his presence and actions testify to his silent love for Mary and her Son. And, while Joseph is, in many ways, only a silent figure standing at the edges of these well-known gospel stories, he is an essential part of the Advent mysteries.

As a "righteous man," Joseph would have been a devout observer of Jewish law and custom, a faith which he would have dutifully handed on to Jesus. But Joseph's relationship with Jesus was that of a father to his son and, as Lucien Deiss, C.Ss.P., has observed, "The most beautiful and truest thing we can say on this topic is that Joseph was so good, so tenderly lovable that as a child Jesus learned to discover in him the heavenly Father's image."[18] (from *Joseph, Mary, Jesus*).

Like Joseph, each of us is called to trust that what God has promised us will be given to us. Beyond this, however, we are also called to obedience—the willingness to listen with the "ear of our heart" which Joseph embodied. The fear and frustration he might have experienced because of Mary's pregnancy or the angel's command gave way to love and an openness of mind and heart that allowed him to see with the eyes of faith the gift God had given to him and to the world.

Readings:
Jeremiah 23:5-8 • Matthew 1:18-25

December 19 • O Root of Jesse's Stem
The Holy Angels

The woman went and told her husband,
"A man of God came to me;
he had the appearance of an angel of God,
terrible indeed.
I did not ask where he came from,
nor did he tell me his name.
But he said to me,
'You will be with child and will bear a son…
The boy shall be consecrated to God from the
*   womb.'"*

—Judges 13:6-7

S acred Scripture and Christian tradition provide us with an understanding of angels that far surpasses our culture's caricature of these divine beings. First, the angels stand before God, giving God honor by virtue of their very existence (cf. Matthew 18:10). Second, angels are messengers, bringing the needs of humanity to God, watching over us: "The Angels speak to man of what constitutes his true being, of what in his life is so often concealed and buried. They bring him back to himself, touching him on God's behalf" (Pope Benedict XVI, *Homily* for September 29, 2007).

The account of the birth of Samson (Judges 13:2-7), the angel's visit to the father of John the Baptist (Luke 1:5-25), and Mary's encounter with Gabriel at the time of the annunciation (Luke 1:26-38) are all signs of God's care and abiding presence with us. And these same angels that stand before God's throne, stand in front of us. Speaking with God, they speak to us.

Our God, the God who speaks to us through his messengers, wants us to believe in peace, in love, in him. As Karl Barth said, "Even if we have never seen angels 'on the right of the incense altar,' the fire of God can actually burn us, the earthquake of God can still shake us, the flood of God can rush around us, the storm of God actually wants to seize us. Oh, if we could actually hear, if we could but hear this voice that resounds so clearly within us as actually God's voice. If only we could believe."[19]

These days before Christmas are a time of watchful awareness. It is also a time of prophecy and proclamation—a duty that has been entrusted to us, who are called to be *angels* ourselves.

Readings:
Judges 13:2-7, 24-25a • Luke 1:5-25

December 20 • O Key of David
Saints Anne and Joachim

Who can ascend the mountain of the Lord?
Or who may stand in his holy place?
He whose hands are sinless, whose heart is clean...
He shall receive a blessing from the LORD,
A reward from God his savior.

—Psalm 24:3-4ab

I n the Sermon on the Mount, Jesus proclaimed, "Blessed are the pure of heart, for they shall see God" (Matthew 5:8). In this sense, purity of heart means more than simply avoiding sin (i.e. being "pure"). Its broadest, fullest meaning involves cultivating a spirit of simplicity and focus: "Remain simple and innocent, and you will be like little children who do not know the evil that destroys man's life" (*Shepherd of Hermas*, Mandate 2:1). Being pure of heart means to focus our attention, our thoughts, and our desires on God's holiness and to allow ourselves to be filled with God's love.

The most perfect expression of this kind of purity is to be found in the virginal heart of Mary, which Caryll Houselander tells us is characterized by emptiness:

"It is not a formless emptiness, a void without meaning; on the contrary it has a shape, a form given to it by the purpose for which it is intended.

It is emptiness like the hollow of a reed, the narrow riftless emptiness, which can have only one destiny: to receive the piper's breath and to utter the song that is in his heart... She was the reed through which the Eternal Love was to be piped as a shepherd's song."

Tradition tells us that Mary's parents, Joachim and Anne, were righteous, hope-filled believers, who prayed that God would grant them a child in their old age. Mary was God's gift to them and it was Joachim and Anne who formed Mary to be a woman of faith. Saint John Paul II reminds us, "On the threshold of the New Testament, it is precisely Joachim and Anne who prepare for the Messiah's coming by welcoming Mary as a gift of God and offering to the world as the immaculate 'ark of salvation'" (*Angelus*, July 25, 1999).

Mary, together with Anne and Joachim, and innumerable saints through the ages, have embodied the hope and trust that are so essential to the Christian life. The faith-filled longing of Anne and Joachim allowed them to become important, although hidden, participants in the salvation of the world. In these final days of Advent, as we begin to celebrate Christmas, keep watching and waiting so that you can truly welcome Christ with a pure heart.

Readings:
Isaiah 7:10-14 • Luke 1:26-38

December 21 • O Radiant Dawn
The Prophets

My love speaks; he says to me,
"Arise, my beloved, my dove, my beautiful one,
    and come!"
"For see, the winter is past,
the rains are over and gone.
The flowers appear on the earth,
the time of pruning the vines has come,
and the song of the dove is heard in our land."
                                    —Song of Songs 2:10-12

Through the ages, God gradually revealed himself to humanity. Beginning with creation itself, and the movements of the human heart, and then, later, through signs and wonders, God invited humankind into a relationship of intimate communion. Although this relationship was broken by the sin of our first parents, God immediately established a new covenant and offered the promise of salvation (cf. Genesis 3).

Through the prophets, God formed his people in hope, "in the expectation of a new and everlasting Covenant intended for all, to be written on their hearts." (*Catechism of the Catholic Church*, 64).[20] The prophets were not fortune-tellers. In many ways, it could be said, the future was only a secondary concern. The prophets were called by God to look at the world around them and to recognize how God was at work in the lives of his people. In times of war, exile, famine, prosperity, or plague, the prophets tirelessly proclaimed a message of salvation. This is embodied in the preaching of the great prophets (Isaiah, Jeremiah, Ezekiel, and Daniel), the "minor" prophets (such as Micah, Haggai, Baruch, and Zechariah), and, finally, John the Baptist. Women, like Sarah, Rebecca, Miriam, Deborah, Judith, and Esther, also played an essential part in keeping alive Israel's hope for salvation.

Advent, it can be said, is the season of prophets. And yet, we need prophets now, more than ever. The prophets were messengers of salvation who watched for the coming of dawn's light into a dark and violent world. Advent calls us to a prophetic wakefulness, challenging us to look at the world around us with the eyes of faith, seeing beyond external appearances to recognize the Spirit at work in the hidden places, especially the human heart: "Let us then live in today's Advent, for it is the time of promise. To eyes that do not see, it still seems that the final dice are being cast down in these valleys, on these battlefields… Those who are awake sense the working of the other powers and can await the coming of their hour."[21]

Readings:
Song of Songs 2:8-14 or Zephaniah 3:14-18a •
Luke 1:39-45

December 22 • O King of All Nations
The Blessed Virgin Mary

His mercy is from age to age
to those who fear him.
He has shown might with his arm,
dispersed the arrogant of mind and heart.
He has thrown down the rulers from their thrones
but lifted up the lowly.

—Luke 1:50-52

O ur tradition has ascribed many titles to
Mary. But I don't believe there are many
of us who would call the Mother of God
a revolutionary. But in her *Magnificat*, which is
re-told in today's Gospel, we hear Mary speaking
as a prophet: The One who has done great things
in and for her is also changing the order of the
world. The poor will be lifted up, the hungry will
be fed, and the least of all the peoples will be
glorified. There is no embrace of the *status quo*
in her words. Instead, they celebrate the seismic
shift that the Incarnation caused in hearts and in

the world itself. John Howard Yoder, a Mennonite theologian, describes Mary's words in this way: "What it says is the language, not of sweet maidens, but of Maccabees: it speaks of dethroning the mighty and exalting the lowly, of filling the hungry and sending the rich away empty. Mary's praise of God is a revolutionary battle cry."

Mary's words were fulfilled in the ministry of her Son, the Divine Physician and Good Shepherd, who came to save those who were deemed least in eyes of the world. And, in spiritual terms, Yoder continues, Mary was rejoicing in "gospel."[22]

In this sense, "gospel" doesn't mean the time-tested and Church-approved account of the life of Jesus. Originally not a religious word, *evangelion* was a secular term for "good news." But this news wasn't just a welcome piece of information. Instead, this "good news" was the report brought by a messenger that a distant battle had been won and that freedom had been preserved; it could also mean that a son had been born to a king, securing stability for the realm. So, "gospel" is good news that affects our welfare.

In these final days before Christmas, Mary's revolutionary song of praise reminds us—in no uncertain terms—why this long-awaited child was coming into the world. This is truly Good News because he is bringing freedom and peace to a war-weary world. And our world today needs to hear this revolutionary call for peace: peace in our communities, our parishes, our homes, and, most especially, in our hearts.

May Mary, the Queen of Peace, continue to inspire us to create a space of welcome for the one who is the Prince of Peace.

Readings:
1 Samuel 1:24-28 • Luke 1:46-58

December 23 • O Emmanuel
Saint John the Baptist

Thus says the Lord GOD:
Lo, I am sending my messenger
To prepare the way before me…
Lo, I will send you
Elijah, the prophet,
Before the day of the LORD comes,
The great and terrible day.

—Malachi 3:23-24

The words of the Prophet Malachi come at the very end of the Old Testament and, as Richard Rohr, O.F.M., observes, they form a perfect segue to the New Testament:

"They describe the one who will be the fitting precursor for any coming Messiah. Christians have, of course, usually applied this passage to John the Baptist, as Jesus himself and the Gospel writers already had done... [Malachi] describes the work of the God Messenger as both 'great and terrible,' both wonderful and threatening at the same time. It is not that the Word of God is threatening us with fire and brimstone, but rather it is saying that *goodness is its own reward and evil is its own punishment.*"[23]

However much we might want it to be otherwise, the prayers and Readings of the Mass for December 23 remind us that we are still in Advent. And the words of Malachi highlight for us the power of the One who is to come:

> And suddenly there will come to the temple /
>   the Lord whom you seek,
>   and the messenger of the covenant whom
>   you desire.
> Yes, he is coming, says the Lord of hosts.
> But who will endure the day of his coming?
>   And who can stand when he appears?
> For he is like a refiner's fire, or like the
>   fuller's lye.

Although most Christians celebrate December 25 as the "birthday" of Jesus, the liturgy in the final days of Advent challenges us to really reflect on the One whom we will welcome in a special way as we celebrate Christmas. Christmas is not only about recalling the birth of Jesus two thousand years ago, but it's also about recognizing how Christ comes to us in so many mysterious ways in our own time and celebrates how he will come again in glory at the end of time.

Throughout this Holy Season, the great prophet John the Baptist has continued to point out for us the One who is the Lamb of God (cf. John 1:29-30): Emmanuel.

In these final hours of waiting, ask John the Baptist, the "prophet of the Most High" (Luke 1:76), to help you be worthy to welcome the Promised One at Christmas.

Readings:
Malachi 3:1-4, 23-24 • Luke 1:57-66

December 24 • Christmas Eve
The Ancestors of Jesus

Through his prophets he promised of old
that he would save us from our enemies,
from the hands of all who hate us.
He promised to show mercy to our fathers
and to remember his holy covenant…
In the tender compassion of our God
the dawn from on high shall break upon us,
to shine on those who dwell in darkness
and the shadow of death,
and to guide their feet into the way of peace.
                                    —Luke 1:70-72, 78-79

The story of our salvation is a story of trees.

Beginning in the Garden of Eden, God placed a tree from which Adam and Eve were forbidden to take the fruit (cf. Genesis 2:16-17). This tree, the Tree of the Knowledge of Good and Evil, became the great sign of humankind's fall from original grace. But, this original sin wasn't that our first parents ate the fruit of this tree; the sin was their disobedience: "In that sin man *preferred* himself to God and by that very act scorned him. He chose himself over and against God... Constituted in a state of holiness, man was destined to be fully 'divinized' by God in glory. Seduced by the devil, he wanted to 'be like God,' but 'without God, before God, and not in accordance with God'" (*Catechism of the Catholic Church*, 398, quoting Saint Maximus the Confessor).

In the fullness of time, however, a new tree would become the great means and sign of our salvation: the Cross. Through his obedience and death on the Cross, Jesus undid the sin of our first parents. As Saint Paul observed, "Just as through one transgression condemnation came upon all, so through one righteous act acquittal and life came to all. For just as through the disobedience of one person the many were made sinners, so through the obedience of the one the many will be made righteous" (Romans 5:18-20). Here we are given an insight into the true meaning of Christmas and the Incarnation: the salvation and renewal of fallen humanity.

But, standing between these two trees—the tree of the Garden and the tree of the Cross—is the powerful symbol of the Tree of Jesse.

A medieval image, the Tree of Jesse depicts the generations of the ancestors of Jesus, with the great prophets and kings of Israel who looked forward to the coming of the Messiah. These ancestors of Jesus are also our spiritual ancestors and we owe them a debt of thanks. Pope Francis reminded us of this in his General Audience on June 25, 2014:

> "If we believe, if we know how to pray, if we acknowledge the Lord and can listen to his Word, if we feel him close to us and recognize him in our brothers and sisters, it is because others, before us, lived the faith and then transmitted it to us. We have *received* faith from our fathers and mothers, from our ancestors, and they have instructed us in it."

As I conclude this series of Advent reflections, in which we've journeyed through Advent with the saints, it only seemed fitting to end by looking back at those who looked forward.

And so, in these final hours of Advent, as we anticipate sunset on Christmas Eve and the beginning of the Christmas Feast, let the powerful symbol of the "Jesse Tree" remind you of the countless generations of faithful women and men who hoped and watched for the coming of Mary's Child. Ask them to help you persevere in your faith and obedience every day of the year.

Readings:
2 Smauel 7:1-5, 8b-12, 14a, 16 • Luke 1:67-79

December 25
The Solemnity of the Nativity of the Lord

A holy day has dawned upon us.
Come, you nations, and adore the Lord.
For today a great light has come upon the earth.
　　—Gospel Verse for the Mass During the Day

I f we truly pay attention to the Church's prayers and the Scripture readings we hear throughout the Christmas Season, we quickly realize that what we are celebrating in these holy days is much more than the "birthday" of Jesus.

In fact, the truth that is at the heart of Christmas is that God became a human being: "the Word became flesh and made his dwelling among us, and we saw his glory, the glory as of the Father's only Son, full of grace and truth" (John 1:14). This belief is so essential that to deny it, or to try to explain it away, is to give up *the* foundational belief of Christians. The Solemnity of Christmas invites us to pause and reflect on what these words really mean.

And so, we recognize that it is one thing to simply say the words "and by the Holy Spirit was incarnate of the Virgin Mary and became man" (from the *Nicene Creed*). It is quite another to allow these words to effect a change in our lives. This is why Cardinal Basil Hume observed, "The words are simple and direct, but their meaning is far beyond our power to comprehend... But it is not flesh and blood that leads us to the truth. It is our Father in heaven who gives us the light to say 'I do believe' and with conviction. His touch is gentle. There is no force as he moves us to share his secret thoughts. He, Emmanuel, is God among us, a man to lead us where we truly belong, wrapped in his love for us."[24]

God's grace has been revealed for the salvation of all humankind. The whole earth sings a new song to the Lord; his glory must be proclaimed to all nations and peoples "for he comes to rule the earth" (Psalm 96:13).

To say that Jesus is Emmanuel—*God-With-Us*—is a profound and dynamic statement of faith. But it is only faith which allows us, like the shepherds and sages of so many centuries ago, to make our way through the darkness to make our way to the manger. War, disease, poverty, the senseless loss of innocent life, can make us ask "Where is God?" But what we, as people of faith, celebrate in the days of Christmas is the reality that God is here, present among us.

Ultimately, as Henri Nouwen wrote, Christmas means saying "Yes" to something beyond emotions and feelings. It is saying "Yes" to hope and the knowledge that salvation is God's work, not ours: "The world is not whole… But it is into this broken world that a child is born, who is called Son of the Most High, Prince of Peace, Savior. I look at him and pray, 'Thank you, Lord, that you came… Your heart is greater than mine'"[25] (*The Road to Daybreak*).

Readings:

Vigil Mass: Isaiah 62:1-5 • Acts 13:16-17, 22-25 •
Matthew 1:1-25
Mass at Midnight: Isaiah 9:1-6 • Titus 2:11-14 •
Luke 2:1-14
Mass at Dawn: Isaiah 62:11-12 • Titus 3:4-7 •
Luke 2:15-20
Mass During the Day: Isaiah 52:7-10 •
Hebrews 1:1-6 • John 1:1-18

Days of Special Celebrations

November 30
The Feast of Saint Andrew the Apostle

Your words, Lord, are Spirit and life.

—John 6:63

Like many of the other Apostles, Andrew is a somewhat obscure figure whose life is shrouded in legend. Scripture tells us that he was a fisherman and a disciple of John the Baptist. He also became the first to answer "yes" to Jesus' invitation to follow him. For this reason, he is honored as the *Protoclete*—the "First-Called." The *Gospel of John* also tells us that after Andrew heard John the Baptist declare that Jesus was "the Lamb of God," he introduced his brother Simon (Peter) to Jesus (cf. John 1:36-40).

While the other gospels tell the story of Andrew's calling a bit differently, we can be confident that Andrew was undoubtedly a man of faith and hope who was willing to leave behind his profession and way of life to follow Jesus. Andrew also demonstrated his faith when he brought to Jesus a young boy with five barley loaves and two fish—simple elements which Jesus transformed into enough food to feed a vast multitude (cf. John 6:8-9).

Andrew was also with Jesus on the Mount of the Transfiguration and with him during his final hours in the Garden of Gethsemane. Ancient traditions tell us that, after Jesus ascended to Heaven and the Holy Spirit came among the Apostles at Pentecost, Andrew preached the Gospel in many places before being martyred in Patras, Greece, by being crucified on a cross in the form of an X.

During the Season of Advent, we renew our commitment to watch and listen as we await the Lord's coming. Saint Andrew is a powerful witness to the truth that our waiting is never in vain: God's promises are always kept and when we are willing to respond to the invitation to be a more dedicated follower of Jesus, our lives are forever transformed into something greater than we would have ever imagined for ourselves.

Readings:
Romans 10:9-18 • Matthew 4:18-22

December 8
The Solemnity of the Immaculate Conception of the Blessed Virgin Mary

Sing to the LORD a new song,
for he has done marvelous deeds.

—Psalm 98:1

When, in 1854, Blessed Pope Pius IX solemnly defined the Dogma of the Immaculate Conception of the Blessed Virgin Mary, he was giving full voice to an ancient and venerable tradition: "The Virgin Mary, in the first moment of her conception, by a singular privilege granted by Almighty God, in view of the merits of Jesus Christ, the Savior of the human race, was preserved free from all stain of original sin" (*Ineffabilis Deus*).

Although it might seem out-of-place to interrupt the quiet, dark procession of the days of Advent with today's joyous celebration of the Immaculate Conception, this solemnity, as Henri Nouwen has observed, embodies the promise of

Advent. "In this feast," he writes, "it seems that all the quiet beauty of Advent suddenly bursts forth into exuberance and exultation. In Mary we see all the beauty of Advent concentrated. She is one in whom the waiting of Israel is most wholly and purely manifested; she is the last of the remnant of Israel for whom God shows his mercy and fulfills his promises; she is the faithful one who believed that the promise made to her by the Lord would be fulfilled; she is the lowly handmaid, the obedient servant, the quiet contemplative. She indeed is the most prepared to receive the Lord."[26]

Our devotion to the Mother of God, expressed in both liturgical and private prayer, celebrates the part Mary played in the decisive moments of salvation history. Her holiness, already fully realized at her Immaculate Conception, but increasing even more through her obedience and cooperation in the work of her Son, is an image of the holiness of the Church, the "spotless Bride of Christ" (*Preface* for the Solemnity of the Immaculate). As Thomas Merton reflected, "The light that shines in Mary is the same light that is to shine in the whole Church and in the entire cosmos recapitulated in Christ. So Mary is compared with the heavenly Jerusalem: 'The Lord has shown us the heavenly Jerusalem filled with the light of God, and her light is like crystal and precious stones' (Revelation 21:10-11)."[27]

Readings:
Genesis 3:9-15, 20 • Ephesians 1:3-6, 11-12 • Luke 1:26-38

December 12
The Feast of Our Lady of Guadalupe

Blessed are you, holy Virgin Mary, deserving of
  all praise;
From you rose the sun of justice, Christ.

—Gospel Verse for
the Feast of Our Lady of Guadalupe

O ne of the most honored titles of the Mother of God is *Star of the Sea*. Derived from the name of Mary, this title emphasizes her role as a sign of hope and as a guiding star for Christians. The Great Cistercian writer, Saint Aelred of Rievaulx, reflected that, "We ought to lift up our eyes to this Star that has appeared on earth today in order that she may lead us, in order that she may enlighten us, in order that she may show us the steps so that we shall know them, in order that she may help us so that we may be able to ascend" (*Sermon 24 on the Nativity of Mary*, 20). The Mother of God, who is also our Mother, receives us into her care, leading us to her Son.

While Saint Aelred's words were written nearly 400 years before the Virgin Mary appeared to Saint Juan Diego Cuauhtlatoatzin, on a hill near Mexico City, in December 1531, they capture something of the important role that the Blessed Virgin played in the evangelization of the New World. Since that time, devotion to Our Lady of Guadalupe has been a mainstay for Catholics in Mexico and throughout the Americas. She has been honored as a patron of the oppressed, a guardian of human life, and a sign of God's provident care for the least of his children.

A 16th-century folksong conveys a sense of the joy and vibrancy that characterize the faith and trust of those who place their confidence in *La Morenita*:

I took delight in all the many-colored flowers,
 so sweet-smelling
that, startled and magnificent, were scattering,
with petals half-opened, in your presence,
 O Mother.

Our Holy Mary.
Your spirit, O Holy Mary, is alive in this picture.
We men praised her,

taking after the Great Book, and danced the
  perfect dance.

And you, Bishop, our father, preached there
by the shore of the lake.

O! I would live securely there.

During these days of Advent-expectation, as we await the coming of the Light, we can take comfort in the words which the Mother of God is said to have addressed to Juan Diego: "Hear me, my littlest one. Let nothing discourage you, nothing depress you. Let nothing alter your heart or your countenance… Am I not your mother? Are you not under the protection of my mantle?"

Readings:
Zechariah 2:14-17 or
Revelation 11:19a; 12:1-6a, 10ab •
Luke 1:26-38 or 39-47

Silas S. Henderson serves as the managing editor of *Abbey Press Publications and* Deacon Digest *magazine. He is the author of the books* From Season to Season: A Book of Saintly Wisdom *and* Moving Beyond Doubt, *as well as numerous* CareNotes, PrayerNotes, *and reflections on prayer and spirituality for numerous Catholic publications.*

NOTES:

[1] Quoted in *Watch for the Light: Readings for Advent and Christmas,* Maryknoll, NY, Orbis Books, 2001. 1.

[2] *The Liturgical Year: The Spiraling Adventure of the Spiritual Life* by Joan Chittister, O.S.B., Nashville, TN, Thomas Nelson, Inc., 2009. 61.

[3] Taken from *The Fathers on the Sunday Gospels* edited by Stephen Mark Holme, Collegeville, MN, The Liturgical Press, 2012. 80-81.

[4] *Rule of Saint Benedict: The Prologue.* Selections in this entry are taken from *Saint Benedict's Rule for Monasteries* translated from the Latin by Leonard J. Doyle, Collegeville, MN, The Liturgical Press, 1984/2001.

[5] Quoted in *Watch for the Light*, 77.

[6] *Grieving at Christmastime* by Dwight Daniels, St. Meinrad, IN, Abbey Press Publications, 2005.

[7] See *Treatise On Contemplation* by Bl. William of Saint-Thierry, quoted in *The Liturgy of the Hours, Volume IV*, 272.

[8] From the essay "Advent as a Penitential Season" by William Stringfellow, quoted in *Watch for the Light,* 104.

[9] *Seasons of Celebration* by Thomas Merton, New York, NY, Farrar, Straus and Giroux, 1965. 88-89.

[10] *The Hidden Life: Essays, Meditations, Spiritual Texts* by Edith Stein (edited by L. Gelber and Michael Linssen, O.C.D. and translated by Waltraut Stein), Washington, D.C., ICS Publications, 1992. 93.

[11] See "On Mary the Egyptian and Zosimus" by Flodoard of Rheims in *Saint Mary of Egypt: Three Medieval Lives in Verse* translated by Hugh Feiss and Ronal Peppin, Kalamazoo, MI, Cistercian Publications, 2005. 64.

[12] Taken from "Christmas Novena" in *From the Heart of Saint Alphonsus: Favorite Devotions From the Doctor of Prayer* edited by Norman J. Muckerman, Liguori, MO, Liguori Publications, 2002. 76.

[13] See *The City of God (De Civitas Dei* 19, 13, 1) by St. Augustine of Hippo (translated by Gerard Walsh *et al.* and edited by Vernon J. Bourke), New York, NY, Doubleday, 1958. 456.

[14] *The Mystery of Love* by Basil Hume, O.S.B., Brewster, MA, Paraclete Press, 2002. 35.

[15] See *Sermon 160* by St. Peter Chrysologus, quoted in *Liturgy of the Hours, Volume I,* 577.

[16] From the essay "The Spirituality of Waiting" by Henri Nouwen, quoted in *Watch for the Light,* 27-36.

[17] From the essay "Evensong" by Gail Godwin, quoted in *Watch for the Light,* 166.

[18] *Joseph, Mary, Jesus* by Lucien Deiss, C.Ss.P., Collegeville, MN, The Liturgical Press, 1996. 20.

[19] From "Lukas 1:5-23" by Karl Barth (translated by Robert J. Sherman), quoted in *Watch for the Light,* 136-137.

[20] See also Isaiah 2:2-4, Jeremiah 31:31-34, and Hebrews 10:16.

[21] From *Advent of the Heart: Seasonal Sermons and Prison Writings* by Alfred Delp, S.J., San Francisco, CA, Ignatius Press, 2006. 30.

[22]From the essay "The Original Revolution" by John Howard Yoder, quoted in *Watch for the Light,* 120-121.

[23]*Preparing for Christmas: Daily Meditations for Advent* by Richard Rohr, O.F.M., Cincinnati, OH, Franciscan Media, 2008.

[24]*The Mystery of the Incarnation* by Basil Hume, O.S.B., London, England, Darton, Longman & Todd, 2004. 142.

[25]*Eternal Seasons: A Spiritual Journey Through the Church's Year* by Henri Nouwen (edited by Michael Ford), Notre Dame, IN, Ave Maria Press, 2007. 58-59.

[26]Ibid, 47.

[27]*New Seasons of Celebration,* 165.